To turtles and turtle protectors everywhere
– Deborah, Ricky-John, Michael, James and Elizabeth

For Siobhan
– James

A catalogue record for this book is available from the National Library of Australia

ISBN: 9781486320288 (hbk)
ISBN: 9781486320295 (epdf)
ISBN: 9781486320301 (epub)

Published by:
CSIRO Publishing
36 Gardiner Road, Clayton VIC 3168
Private Bag 10, Clayton South VIC 3169
Australia

Telephone: +61 3 9545 8400
Email: publishing.sales@csiro.au
Website: www.publish.csiro.au
Sign up to our email alerts: publish.csiro.au/earlyalert

Edited by Belinda Bolliger
Cover, text design and layout by Cath Pirret Design
Printed in China by Toppan Leefung Printing Limited

CSIRO acknowledges the Traditional Owners of the lands that we live and work on across Australia and pays its respect to Elders past and present. CSIRO recognises that Aboriginal and Torres Strait Islander peoples have made and will continue to make extraordinary contributions to all aspects of Australian life including culture, economy and science. The use of Western science in this publication should not be interpreted as diminishing the knowledge of plants, animals and environment from Indigenous ecological knowledge systems.

Note for readers: A glossary can be found at the back of the book.

Note for teachers: Teacher notes are available at: https://www.publish.csiro.au/book/8222/#forteachers

Aug25_01

MYSTERY OF THE MISSING TURTLES

Deborah S. Bower, Ricky-John Spencer, Michael B. Thompson, James U. Van Dyke and Elizabeth Hale

Illustrated by James O'Hanlon

PUBLISHING

Brooke loved exploring the creek at the bottom of her farm. She loved basking with skinks, picnicking with wallabies and climbing trees to watch birds.

Every day Brooke kept a notebook.
She wrote about darters chasing fish,
rakali eating mussels, and yabbies munching plants.
But her favourite animals ...

... were the freshwater turtles.

There were long-necked turtles with pretty yellow-and-black shells, broad-shelled turtles with flat heads peering out of the water ...

... and Murray River turtles with pale-striped faces. Some of them were big and some were huge!

Brooke found turtles eating yabbies,
turtles basking on logs,
turtles popping up to breathe.

But everywhere she looked,
all the turtles were big and old.

Where were the baby turtles?

As the summer grew hotter,
the river red gum began to flower.

The banjo frogs started calling loudly.
The platypuses were pairing up.
The water dragon mum was swollen with eggs.

Brooke found a turtle nest.
There was just one problem though ...
a thief had eaten the eggs!

There were clues left in the sand, but Brooke was not sure who or what had left them. She had to find out what had happened to the turtle eggs.

Brooke collected some chicken eggs and dug them into the ground. She disguised them as a turtle nest to trick the criminal.

She and her dad placed a trail camera in front of the eggs. She hoped the criminal would take the bait overnight.

The next morning, Brooke's nest had been dug up.

She checked the camera and saw
a fat red fox. This was the thief who
was eating all the eggs!

Brooke understood why she could not find any baby turtles.

The fox was eating the eggs before the baby turtles could hatch.

Brooke was worried that if no nests survived, one day there would be no turtles left.

But what could she do to save them?

Brooke became a detective.

She found where the turtles were nesting
and every day she set her trail camera
near the nests.

She asked her dad to lend her some pegs and wire from his fence and built a grid to place over each nest.

Each morning Brooke checked the camera.

She could see that the fox was visiting during the night, but he couldn't get through the wire grid to the eggs.

Her plan was working!

Early one morning, as the air felt cool and the honeyeater was fledging, Brooke saw movement in the bank.

A baby turtle popped out of the dirt. Its brothers and sisters followed close behind.

Brooke guarded the baby turtles from hungry kookaburras and ravens as they made their way down to the creek.

She counted as the turtles came out of the nest ...
Fifteen, sixteen, seventeen!

Over the next week, the eggs in the protected nests hatched and 100 baby turtles crawled down to the creek.

Brooke and her dad built a fence so that the whole bank was protected from foxes and the turtles could nest safely.

Now when Brooke explores the creek, she counts as many young turtles as old turtles, swimming and basking happily together.

TURTLE POWER

Australian turtles

Australia has about 30 species of turtles. Each species is different and has adapted to the environment around it. There are 24 species of side-necked turtles, like the ones in our story. They live in freshwater wetlands and rivers from the tip of Cape York in Far North Queensland, down to South Australia and across to Perth in Western Australia. These turtles include species with very long necks that move side to side (hence the name) and do not completely retract into their shells.

The pig-nosed turtle is a unique species that lives in the seasonally flowing rivers of the Top End, basking in the warm spring water that rises from deep underground. The six largest species of Australian turtles live in the salty ocean and can travel long distances around the world.

Worrisome woes

Turtles grow slowly over many years. It can be 10 years or more before they start making babies, and many baby turtles are eaten by other animals such as fish and birds. That means that once turtles become adults, they need to live a long time to replace themselves in the population. Such a life-history strategy leaves turtles vulnerable to extinction in today's world. Many changes to the environment are threatening turtles. Introduced species, like foxes and pigs, dig up turtle nests to eat the eggs and also hunt and eat adults. Fences are a problem when they do not allow turtles to pass through. Turtles can get trapped and become dehydrated and die. In some areas of Australia, taking too much water from rivers for agriculture causes waterholes to dry up and entire turtle populations to die. Over one-third of Australia's turtle species are threatened with extinction.

Turtle or tortoise?

All tortoises are turtles, but not all turtles are tortoises! Turtles are reptiles with a shell that has formed by fusing their rib cage to their backbone. Tortoises spend more time on land but still belong to the wider grouping of turtles. In Australia, many turtles are mistaken for tortoises because they are often seen on land walking from pond to pond. There are over 350 living species of turtles around the world and many more extinct species we have discovered from fossils. Today, our living turtle species include the giant land tortoises of the Galapagos Islands and the soft-shelled river turtles that are built for speed in the water. All the tortoise species belong to this large group we call turtles. Collectively, the scientific name for all these shelled animals is Testudines.

Land and air

Australian turtles spend most of their time in water. For many species, the only time they leave the water is to nest. A female turtle will walk out of the water and find an area of soil where she uses her two back legs to dig a hole. Turtles lay between 10 and 30 eggs in a hole that they cover up and never visit again. Hatchling turtles use an egg tooth to escape from the egg, then dig to the surface and run to the water. Baby turtles work together to dig out of their nests all at the same time. By running to the water in a group, each hatchling reduces its chances of being eaten.

Garbage collectors

Turtles have been on Earth since before the time of the dinosaurs. They can live in oceans and freshwater areas, including lakes, rivers, wetlands, dams and ponds. Turtles eat both plants and other animals. Their diet is important because it helps to keep wetlands clean. When other animals die, turtles eat them, which prevents outbreaks of harmful algae. In this way, they are the garbage collectors of our waterways. Turtles also breathe oxygen from the air, which means they can survive in waterholes where fish cannot. Since their metabolism relies on the temperature around them, turtles can survive much longer without eating than birds or mammals.

Bum breathers

Have you ever been for a swim and wished you could stay under the water to explore the depths below? Turtles have an ingenious solution to do just that. They breathe out of their bum! In fact, many species of freshwater turtles that live in fast-flowing rivers obtain oxygen from breathing air through their nostrils and by pumping water through their bum. Like a fish's gills, turtle bums have very thin skin that absorbs the oxygen dissolved in the water. Bum breathing means they can save energy and stay below water for longer. A real superpower!

Turtles as pets

Turtles are tiny when they hatch (and extremely cute!). Many people buy them as pets, not realising how large they can grow. It is a big problem when turtles are released into places where they do not belong. Introduced species can compete for food and space with native species and bring disease. It is important that abandoned turtles are given to wildlife carers and not released into the wild. It's even better to find and watch turtles in nature and help wild populations to survive on their own.

Becoming a turtle warrior with '1 Million Turtles'

Anyone can help research and save turtles by joining our program, 1 Million Turtles. We created 1 Million Turtles so you can be involved in conserving turtles too. We provide resources and training on our website, **1millionturtles.com**. You can learn to protect a turtle nest, build a turtle island or complete a predation survey. Our citizen scientists are recording data through TurtleSAT, **turtlesat.org.au**, where you can track the location of turtles and their nests. There's also an app version for your mobile phone. If you see a basking turtle, a turtle crossing the road or turtle eggshells broken on the ground, you can join our turtle warriors by recording your discovery. We are using this information to identify where turtles need better protection from foxes, car traffic or other hazards. The information also helps to predict where turtles are nesting and to discover new places where turtles live. Keep your eyes open for turtles and help them on their way if you can. If everyone helps to protect one turtle, soon one million turtles will be saved and these amazing animals can continue to benefit Earth for many more years to come.

GLOSSARY

Adapted: When animal or plant species change over time to survive in their environment.

Agriculture: Farming and growing crops or raising animals for food, clothing and other products.

Algae: Plant-like organisms that live in water. They can grow very quickly and may become toxic and use up oxygen in the water (harmful algae).

Basking: When an animal rests in a warm spot, such as a rock or the shore, to warm up and stay warm.

Citizen scientists: People of any age and ability who help collect information about animals and nature.

Dehydrated: When a living thing doesn't have enough water in its body and starts to feel weak or sick.

Egg tooth: A small, hard tooth on the tip of a hatchling's snout that helps it break open the eggshell when it hatches. After hatching, the egg tooth is no longer needed and falls off.

Extinction: When there are no more animals, plants or species of a certain kind left anywhere in the world.

Fossils: Old bones or imprints of plants and animals that have turned to stone over time. Fossils help us learn about creatures from long ago.

Freshwater: Water that is not salty, such as water in lakes and rivers.

Introduced species: Animals or plants that humans have brought to a place where they do not naturally live. Sometimes they can cause problems for native wildlife.

Mammals: A group of related animals that usually have fur or hair and whose mothers produce milk. You are a mammal. Cats, platypuses, kangaroos and whales are all examples of mammals too.

Metabolism: How animals turn food into energy. When a turtle is cold, its metabolism is slow, so it can go a long time without eating. Our metabolism is fast, so we get hungry just a few hours after a meal.

Oxygen: The part of the air that people, animals and plants need to live. We breathe in oxygen to help our bodies work.

Predation: When one animal hunts, catches and eats another animal for food; for example, a lion catching a zebra or a frog eating a fly.

Species: A group of animals that is similar and can have babies together. There are many species of turtles.

Testudines: The scientific name for all turtles and tortoises.

Wetlands: Areas where the land is covered with shallow water, such as swamps and marshes. Wetlands are important for many animals.

Wildlife carers: People who help sick or injured wild animals and take care of them until they are ready to return to the wild.

ACKNOWLEDGEMENTS

This story was conceived and written on Anēwan land and inspired by Dr Brooke Kennedy, a Kamilaroi Indigenous lecturer and scientist. We pay our respects to the first scientists who care for Country and turtles in Australia. A large team contributed to the development of 1 Million Turtles and this book. Special thanks to contributors Sylvia Clarke, Geetha Ortac, Anthony Santoro, Marilyn Connell, Courtney Monk, Atlanta Veld and to the professional and citizen scientists of Australia who have become an immovable force in the fight to protect Australian freshwater turtles from extinction. Personal thanks extend to Professor Arthur Georges, Eric Nordberg, Sarah Reddington, Donald McKnight, Louise Streeting and Siobhan O'Hanlon. Researchers were supported by the University of New England, Western Sydney University and La Trobe University. Funding of the 1 Million Turtles Program was supported by a Department of Industry, Science and Resources Citizen Science grant.